The Art

Improve Your Critical Thinking and Decision Making Skills and Learn How to Solve Problems Creatively

By Michael Sloan

Copyright 2016 by Michael Sloan

Published by Make Profits Easy LLC

Profitsdaily123@aol.com

facebook.com/MakeProfitsEasy

Table of Contents

Introduction: 4
Chapter 1: Overwhelming Problems 7
Chapter 2: How A Problem Solver Thinks 24
Chapter 3: The Discovery Process of Problem Solving 59
Chapter 4: Taking Action 78
Conclusion: 105

Introduction:

We all have problems. Our lives are often bombarded with the constant influx of problems, issues and troubles that plague us, pull us down and make our lives harder. Yet, despite the fact that we all have problems, how often do we really look for solid, concrete ways to solve them?

If you've lived a life of frustration and confusion when it comes to problem solving, have no fear! With the Art of Problem solving, we're going to help you figure out how to take a critical look at your problems. We'll help you analyze them with a rational, measured approach and then solve them in a timely and effective manner.

Problem solving isn't about overthinking, worrying or having anxiety about what bothers you. The act of solving a problem is nothing more than being able to evaluate the size of the problem. To think of what would make for a good response to the problem and then ultimately take the steps required to solve the problem. With this book, we're going to take you on a thorough guide through each of the steps required to be able to solve a problem with ease and efficiency.

Problem solving is far more than just a simple act. It is a mindset that will allow for you to conquer any problem in your path, whether it's big, small or something in-between. Our goal is to help you learn the three simple methods of analyzing any problem and to learn the psychology of a problem solver. Believe it or not, problem solving is more about how you look at the world as opposed to how you handle problems. Over the course of this book we're going to show you how to change your viewpoint on dealing with being overwhelmed, uncomfortable and nervous about the future. Rather than focus on just a few simple steps to solve your problems, we want you to learn that the mindset of being a problem solver is for life! Does that interest you? We hope so, come along with us and take a journey through the process of learning to become a problem solver!

Chapter 1: Overwhelming Problems

Problems come in many different shapes and sizes. When we encounter various problems in our lives, we often respond to them based on our capability to handle them. For example, when you're busy getting your laundry done and you realize you're out of laundry detergent, you've encountered a very simple problem. You know all of the elements involved: you need detergent; you don't have any. You also know the solution to the problem as well, which in this case would be going to the store to buy some more.

Yes, some problems are much more complex. Imagine that as you're driving to the store, you hear a strange humming coming from your car and smoke begins to billow out of it. You end up experiencing an entirely different new type of problem. You know what the problem is, the car is smoking, but you actually don't know exactly how to solve this problem.

When we hit problem areas that we are unable to immediately solve, we can find that we become extremely anxious or frustrated with the issue. Worse, if we aren't even able to readily understand how to solve the problem, we might find ourselves becoming overwhelmed with the situation.

When a person becomes overwhelmed, they'll often have trouble responding to it. Instead of beginning to go through the process of working their way through the problem, the feelings of being overwhelmed causes the individual to shut down in a manner of different ways. Perhaps you've experienced this too.

When overwhelmed, we can often:

- Grow angry with the situation and pointlessly rage about how things don't work out

- Become filled with hopelessness and despair. This leads us to not even bother with the fixing of the problem

- Realize we don't know the answer and grow afraid of the unknown, hesitating in handling it

- Grow apathetic due the complexity and refuse to face the situation head on.

- Put the thing off, hoping that eventually we'll feel less overwhelmed but we never do.

If you've ever dealt with any of these symptoms when trying to solve a problem, you aren't alone. Most people who have to deal with problems will encounter things that they feel are just far too big and complex for them to be able to solve.

Yet, why do we feel so overwhelmed when problems rear their heads? For things that we can readily solve, there isn't much emotional turmoil. If you know how to change a tire and you have a spare, you might feel frustrated at the situation. But when you have a flat tire you aren't overwhelmed because you are able to change the tire. So you kneel down, get the tools out and get to work because you aren't overwhelmed with the situation.

Consequently, if you're someone who has never changed a tire before and you are faced with the dilemma of changing the tire, what happens within us emotionally at that time? We begin to feel fear, frustration, confusion and hopelessness. Sometimes those feelings can actually be so strong that we don't even get to work.

So what is the solution to dealing with the overwhelming sense of fear, confusion, anger or anxiety when dealing with a problem that seems bigger than us? Is it simply a matter of gaining experience in all fields? Is the best way to solve problems to just know about what the problem is ahead of time and have a solution prepared in advanced? No! Not at all. The Art of Problem Solving is conceptual in nature. This means that if you learn the process and the concepts of how to solve problems, you can apply them to just about any situation and it will serve you better. You don't have to be prepared for every single problem in your life to be able to solve them. Realistically, you can't really be prepared for all the obstacles that will come in your way because quite frankly, you don't know what's in store for you! A problem is frustrating because they usually show up uninvited and unexpected.

The good news, however, is that if you are able to understand why you feel overwhelmed when dealing with certain situations. You will be able to work through the feelings and become more capable of the task at hand. Good problem solving isn't just about having a solution to the issue, rather it's about having a process of approach, discovery and solution finding. So let's focus right now on what's known as the approach process, or essentially learning how to sum up the situation at hand.

Approach Step One: Recognize How You Feel

The first step to being able to approach the problem is learning how to recognize exactly what you are feeling. Oftentimes when we become overwhelmed, our minds become overstimulated and we start to experience a lot of emotions at once. This creates sort of a big ball of twine that our feelings get tangled up in. By being able to slow down and process through your emotions one step at a time, you will be able to get a better handle on how to approach the problem.

So it's important to ask yourself what you are feeling and try to come to terms with each emotion. If you're angry, ask yourself why are you angry. If you're sad, ask yourself what is making you sad. Don't just allow all of your emotions to storm up inside of you and create the sensation that you are overwhelmed. Sort through each and every feeling until you have a concrete understanding of each thing that's going on inside of you.

Once you have an understanding of how you feel, it's time for you to stop and ask yourself what you want to do with those feelings. Our feelings are extremely important because they signal important things to us. Fear tells us that we need to be cautious. Anger tells us we need to be protected. Sorrow communicates the idea that something wrong is going on. Your emotions are very good for you, but if we don't have a steady grasp on what they are trying to do, it can be extremely overwhelming.

Think of your emotions like a dog. When you get home, you find your dog barking and jumping up and down excitedly. Let's assume you just bought this dog, so you have no idea what it wants, but the dog just keeps leaping up and down and barking. Your mind will quickly try to decipher all of the information at hand. But the fact is, if you aren't used to working with that dog, you're just going to be stuck guessing at what the barks mean.

Likewise, if you aren't used to working with your own emotions and deciphering what they are trying to tell you, each time you have to deal with an emotional situation, you'll find yourself becoming overwhelmed. By taking the time to recognize each emotion and separate them from one another, you will be able to move forward without that heavy feeling of being overwhelmed.

Approach Step Two: Look at the Problem

After you've spent a good amount of time assessing how you feel emotionally and sorting through the emotions that have reared their head, you are now in the position of being able to look at the problem with an objective state of mind. Please note that we're just talking about looking at the problem right now, we're not talking about solutions yet. Don't try to pull the cart before the horse when it comes to the problem solving process. There are three distinct phases in the process of solving problems, so don't jump to the last phase of solving the problem. It's important to focus on just approaching the problem first.

When it comes to looking at the problem, all you are really doing is making a note of the problem at hand. Take some time to objectively look at what you are facing and figure out every possible detail of the problem.

Approach Step Three: Break the problem down

What can make a problem so overwhelming for us is that the problem itself might seem to be some big, ominous task that requires a massive undertaking. Like our emotions, if we try to look at a problem as just one big jumble we will end up feeling overwhelmed with what's involved. Try not focusing on what is overwhelming and what kind of size the problem is. Try to sit down and break what you are facing down into as many small problems as possible. It's way easier to handle a series of small problems than it is to handle one big one.

For example, let's assume that one big problem that you're facing is debt. Instead of summing up the entire problem just as "I owe $50,000" you can instead break down how much you owe and where into a series of smaller steps. For example, you can break down your debt so it looks like this:

- Car Debt: 15,000
- Credit Card Debt 10,000
- Student Loans 25,000

See, with the action of taking a hard look at your financial problems and breaking it down, you've turned one big problem into three separate problems that are smaller in size. They might still total up to a $50,000 in debt, but by focusing on each piece of the puzzle rather than the whole, you can receive clarity on just exactly what needs to be handled.

The more you focus on breaking a problem down into its elements, the less overwhelmed you will feel about the problem at hand. Most problems aren't anything more than complicated To-Do lists. But because we don't break them down, we become intimidated by the size of what threatens us.

The key to overcoming the overwhelming problems that often scare us into submission isn't trying to solve the problem immediately. Instead, it is being able to look at our own emotional responses. Then see how we feel in the moment and then focus on how we can look directly at the problem without becoming intimidated.

There's an old story about two men, lumberjacks by trade, who come together and decide that they are going to have a contest. Whoever chops the most wood, they agree, within five hours is the winner of the contest. Well, the younger man immediately sets about cutting trees, chopping hour after hour after hour. Eventually when he finishes he proudly looks at the many trees that he felled. He had noticed that the older lumberjack had been sitting idly for a few hours while he was working, so the younger man was confident that he would win the contest.

When the young lumberjack went to brag to the older one, he discovered that the old man had absolutely decimated his side of the forest. He had cut almost twice as many trees in the time that the young man had. Confused and taken aback, the young lumberjack asked "how did you cut so many trees down when I started before you and kept cutting trees down relentlessly?" The old man grinned and replied "Well, I spent one hour cutting down trees, but I spent four hours sharpening my axe."

When it comes to solving problems, the knee jerk reaction is to just jump into figuring out how to have a solution as quickly as possible. The fact is, however, that when we slow our process down and focus on building up a strong method of being able to look at problems and analyze them, we are in the act of sharpening our axes. The goal isn't to be able to solve specific problems, rather the goal is to become a problem solver and that starts with changing your mindset.

Chapter 2: How A Problem Solver Thinks

Problem solving isn't just simply a task, rather it is a way of thinking. The Art of Problem Solving is more about a state of mind than doing any one thing. So how do problem solvers approach life? Well, they approach everything with the concept of discovery in their head. Discovery is the act of being able to sift through information and finding out the things that are relevant to the task at hand. For example, if you were trying to figure out how to fix a flat tire, what would the process of discovery look for?

The first step you're going to take in learning a solution is actually automatic. You're going to fall back on past experiences. If you've fixed flat tires before, your mind is going to quickly take you back to the time where you fixed the tire. It will inform you of all the steps involved. If you had studied on the process of how to fix a flat tire, you would recall that information.

What happens, however, when that automatic search that runs through your mind comes up empty? What do you do when you suddenly realize that you don't have an answer to your question? There are many different responses. Some people will call a knowledgeable friend for assistance while others might consult the internet. Some might just freeze up entirely, unable to figure out the next step in their problem solving path.

The process of beginning to look at solutions is known as the discovery process. There are many different ways to go about discovery, but oftentimes we become very limited in our ability to look for those solutions. What makes it so hard for us to think past these obstacles? Well, oftentimes it's because these obstacles give the appearance that they are somewhat insolvable. The reality isn't that the problem is insurmountable. The reality is that we ourselves can put great limitations on our own abilities.

The mindset of a problem solver, however, isn't one that is concerned with the inability to deal with something. Rather the mindset of the problem solver is much more interested in trying their best to solve the problem at hand. They do this by sifting through all available methods of learning and determining which is the best. In other words, they use the process of discovery until they are able to come to an adequate solution that will ultimately assist them in their goals.

So how do we frame our minds to think in terms of a problem solver? Well, since it's a state of mind, that means if you begin to develop specific habits and patterns of thought. If you constantly work to keep the frame of mind, eventually you will start becoming a problem solver of your own. Let's take a look at some of the mindsets that are behind the thought process of the problem solver.

Problem Solving Mindset One: Confidence in Learning

A problem solver's mind is geared in such a way that they know they have the capacity to learn the answer, even if they don't have the answer readily available. By developing the skill set to learn how to solve a problem, they are capable of figuring out exactly what is necessary to fix the situation. Let's look at a very common form of problem solving: fixing a computer.

When it comes to fixing a computer, most people feel very helpless. Oftentimes they will consult with problem solvers to fix said machine. If their email isn't working or if something goes wrong with the software, a person can be quick to call a friend who is "good with computers." This person who is supposedly good with computers usually has access to one secret that the ordinary personal doesn't know. That secret? Google. Believe it or not, but most computer gurus know that there are potentially thousands of problems that can occur when it comes to computers. There are so many issues at hand that knowing the exact answer to a problem isn't nearly as valuable as knowing how to find the answer.

A computer specialist's job is more about finding the correct solution than knowing it off of the top of his head. When he goes to his friend's house to fix the computer, he most likely is going to either operate purely off of experience if he's seen the issue a few times before or just run a quick search about what the problem is. His ability to use the search function and learn how to solve the problem makes him the most capable individual in that house when it comes to problem solving.

If the distressed computer user would spend time learning the process of going to search for solutions and how to consistently sift through data until a solution was reached, they'd be quite capable of being just as skilled with computers as the specialist.

A problem solver's job isn't to know everything, because frankly that is impossible. Rather the problem solver works to cultivate a mindset of readiness to learn. They focus on gaining the ability to learn instead of trying to just memorize everything necessary to solve a problem. This might seem a little confusing, the idea of learning how to learn. But consider this:

college students who take a class on how to learn will outperform college students who don't take the class over the course of a year.

We often take the concept of learning for granted. It can be incredibly easy to just assume that you know how to learn well and then move onto other, more pressing matters. The fact might be that if you are struggling with the Art of Problem Solving, this could be an education issue. By spending some time learning how to learn well, you will be setting yourself up for success.

A problem solver has confidence in the ability to learn the answer. This essentially takes away one of the most intimidating things a problem often provides: the unknown. If you are confident that you can spend time learning the answer to problems, instead of being confident in your ability to know the problems ahead of time, you don't have to worry about the fear of the unknown. You can just focus on learning the answers to the questions that you have.

Here are some tips for adapting the mindset of Confidence in Learning:

- Never say, I don't know. Rather try to find the answer somehow.

- In today's information driven society, you are far more capable of learning the intimate workings of something just by looking it up online.

- Don't let your lack of education on a subject daunt you. You can spend adequate time learning about the subject through books, online videos, college level courses if you're really committed or just asking a friend who knows about it.

- Humility is the key when it comes to adapting a learning mindset. It takes a certain amount of guts to be able to say, "I don't know the answer." So, in order to truly spend time learning how to solve your problems, you're going to need the humility to learn from other sources about the situation.

Problem Solver Mindset Two: Humility

Have you ever heard of Richard Branson? If not, have you ever heard of Virgin Airlines?

Most likely you have heard about this man and his exploits in business. Richard Branson founded Virgin with a goal of being a multi-faceted corporation that gets involved in many different areas of business. This includes privatized space travel known as Virgin Galactic. This man is a problem solver. Would you like to know what a man with a net worth of 4.9 Billion dollars has to say about the best way to solve problems? "One of the reasons my friends and I were successful early on was because we always asked lots of questions. I was willing to listen to anyone who could help and over the years many people volunteered their advice."

While it is very easy to ask others for input into our ideas and concepts, it can actually be a little harder to just agree and take their advice at face value. Oftentimes when it comes to our own selves, we have to deal with our ego and pride. We are constantly trying to prove that we are capable on our own. Yet a problem solver doesn't give into pride. They are willing to lower themselves through the act of humility and truly consider what others have to tell them.

Just as we talked about learning the ability to gain information on the subject at hand, we would like for you to know that there is a great number of people in this world who can help you in solving your problems. There is a myth that in order to be successful in life we must make it through all of our problems and obstacles alone. That accepting help somehow makes us weaker. In truth, looking to others in our times of need makes us much stronger because we have the assistance of another person to help carry the workload.

It takes humility to reach out to others and ask them for their advice. Saying "I can't figure this out alone" can feel somewhat scary, especially if we have to admit it to our superiors in the workplace. But a problem solver is more interested in solving the issue at hand than keeping his own pride. Think about it, when it comes to solving problems, what is the ultimate goal? Is the goal to feel really good about ourselves and think about how great we are? Or is the goal to actually solve the problem? Someone who refuses to reach out for assistance from others is just trying to feed their own egos. A real problem solver focuses on what needs to be solved and calls out for help quickly and eagerly.

Problem Solver Mindset 3: Resilience

Resilience is the fine art of being able to spring back from a difficulty. The concept of a resilient person would be like the boxer who, after being walloped hard in the face, is able to sufficiently recover from the blow and begin fighting back against his opponent.

A problem solver is resilient in the face of adversity. There are times when a problem solver can become overwhelmed or frustrated. There will be discouragement in the life of a problem solver and they can certainly be tempted to give up. They might even stop trying for a little bit, but in the end they bounce back. They are resilient.

Likewise, if we want to develop the mindset of being a problem solver, it means that we must develop a firm and strong form of resilience. We need an inner strength that allows us to come back from frustrations and poor situations with strength and determination. So how do we develop a resilient mind? Well, it requires discipline and dedication but it also requires a sense of optimism. If you don't have the ability to see that things will get better, how can you ever expect to bounce back?

Problem solving isn't about simply just fixing something. Remember, it is about developing a powerful mindset that allows you to systematically approach any issue in your life and fix it with skill and speed. Attitude is everything when it comes to developing the mindset of the problem solver, because the problem solver must believe that it can be fixed. If you don't have a sense of optimism toward the thing that you are trying to fix, then you will find the situation to be hopeless. Optimism will lead you to become resilient. You can only bounce back if you think you can win.

Think about the boxer, for a moment. When the boxer in the ring gets hit really hard and falls to the ground, he must get up in order to be able to keep fighting. But what if he is laying on the floor, believing that he is unable to win? Why would he ever stand up? Even if he is in intense pain, even if his vision is blurry and his muscles are aching, he must have, above all, optimism and a belief that he can win. Then, and only then, can he bounce back. He can hold to his resilience and stand up to fight back.

Likewise, if we don't have the optimism when looking at our problems, we will never develop the mindset of the problem solver. The problem solver's job is to look at the situation and figure out how he can solve it. But the underlying belief is that the problem *can and will* be solved. If the problem solver were to look at the situation and say "well this is hopeless," then why would they ever go about trying to fix the problem?

At the end of the day, in order to become resilient, we must develop an optimism that things will improve. We must look at the challenges in front of us as solvable and we must look at ourselves as the people who have the capability of solving it.

So how do we build a resilient mindset? How do we learn to bounce back from adversity? Here's a few things to consider:

- Focus on being more flexible with your life. Oftentimes things don't work out the way we've planned and there is a strong temptation to resist what is happening. Rather than panic when you experience changes, try to look at the positives to the change. Learn to adapt to what is happening as opposed to resisting new things.

- Make a point of focusing on the good things in your life, even when dealing with adversity. By developing a position of gratitude, you are inoculating yourself against stress and frustration from having to encounter hardship. Being grateful for where you are in life and having an attitude of looking on the bright side of life will ultimately decrease your stress. This will increase your natural resilience.

- Push yourself physically! Working out and exercising not only has great cardiovascular benefits for your body, but it also helps increase your discipline which grows your resiliency.

- Don't make problems a catastrophe. When you are dealing with a problem, don't obsess over it and don't give it any power over you. By fearing the absolute worst when dealing with a problem, you are essentially letting it grow out of control. Then it starts to affect the way that you live your life. Don't let obsessive thinking drag you down!

Problem Solving Mindset 4: Embracing Challenges

One of the most crucial things that you can learn in the Art of Problem solving is learning to look at challenges as good things rather than things to be avoided. Part of our natural temperature in society today is that we have an innate desire to avoid the bad things in life. When fear rears its head, we like to retreat from the scary thing and hide somewhere safe. It's just the way our culture has raised us. Confrontation and embrace of challenge is on the lower end of the social spectrum. Passive aggressiveness and indirect confrontation, however, appear to be on the rise especially through means of communication such as email, texting and even social media.

The fact is, as a society we are starting to lose our ability to see challenge as a good and healthy thing. Why? Because challenges tend to be uncomfortable. When we experience discomfort, we immediately seek a way to escape from such feelings. This usually involves retreating from the problem at hand. Our current society is very interested in being as comfortable as possible. Convenience is usually one of the most prized possessions in the first world. The things that once were considered luxuries, such as air conditioning and computers have now worked their way into being seen as necessities. Food is readily available at every corner and the idea of skipping a meal is quickly condemned as being extremely unhealthy. The challenges that our ancestors once faced, the hardship of hunting and gathering, living in a rough and dangerous world where shelter was something you had to work hard to build, are no longer around.

Since we as people are no longer forced to live in a constant war for survival, we aren't exposed to the rigors of such challenges. When it came down to hunting, it didn't matter for our ancestors if they were overwhelmed or not. They had to hunt or they would starve to death. The threat of a predator in their midst wasn't something they could just ignore and hope it goes away. Rather they had to deal with the very real confrontation of dealing with a tribal enemy and fighting to survive. There are many benefits to modern society. We should be very thankful that modern industry and convenience allows for us to readily access food, clothing and other necessities without having to deal with the threat of death.

The problem is that there has been nothing to replace the challenges that we once faced back then. As society grows more complex, we are discovering that we have the luxury of avoiding most of our problems. Avoidance, of course, leads to disaster in the long run. Since we are able to feel good in the moment, we often choose to accept immediate gratification as opposed to feeling the discomfort of dealing with challenges.

The problem solver looks at challenges with a willingness to tackle them head on as opposed to trying to circumvent the problem. They don't let their discomfort get the best of them and they don't run away when they feel afraid or worried about a situation. They accept that they have discomfort within them but they don't stop. They embrace the challenges ahead of them as opposed to thinking of the problem as something to avoid entirely.

Our culture puts us at a natural disadvantage when it comes to dealing with discomfort because we often equate discomfort with pain. When something feels bad, we assume that it is hurting us. The reality is that our discomfort is nothing more than a signal that what we are experiencing is unpleasant. Unpleasantness isn't pain, but since we often live our lives in the search for ways to feel better, we often make the mistake of confusing the two.

Are you interested in learning to embrace obstacles in front of you, rather than shrinking away? It is not an easy process; it requires a total shift in perspective to be able to do such a thing.

It's worth it, however, if you are looking to develop the mindset of a problem solver.

So how do we learn to look at obstacles as good things? Well, let's go through each step.

Step One: Change Your Perception of Discomfort

Discomfort is not a bad thing. That tenseness that you feel inside your stomach when you think of asking for that promotion, that gut-wrenching sensation you experience as you ponder asking someone out on a date, all of those feelings are natural reactions to going outside of your comfort zone. Comfort is something that you are used to. It's enjoyable and acceptable. When you are comfortable, there isn't much reason to seek change. Likewise, when you begin to experience discomfort, it is because you are in the process of some sort of change.

Discomfort isn't pain, it is merely the response to change. The problem lies in the fact that when you are experiencing change, you are often giving up something for something else. So suppose that you want to start working out. You will begin to feel a discomfort at having to wake up early each morning so that you can get your work out time. You are experiencing something new, waking up early, and it is markedly different from your old system, which was to wake up later. You might feel an immense discomfort with having to commit your time and energy to doing such a thing. However, in the long run it will actually be very good for you because you will get all of the benefits of working out.

When we begin to take action with ourselves and move outside of what is normal for us, we're going to experience some level of discomfort. If you think that these feelings of discomfort are bad, then you will shrink back and recoil in horror. You will seek a way to escape such feelings and that involves returning back to our comfort zone.

The solution to dealing with discomfort is being able to change how we look at it. Once we've started realizing that discomfort is merely an indicator that things are changing and that you are moving out of something comfortable, we can continue moving forward. If we always look at discomfort as nothing more than a bad thing, it will always hold us back.

Step Two: Realize That Obstacles Are a Part of Growth

When we encounter challenges, we are put in the precarious position of needing the skill sets to overcome them. We might not have the skills necessary to overcome the challenge or obstacle at the beginning of the problem, but if we try to focus and push ourselves to accomplish our goals, we will find ourselves growing as people.

Each time you climb over a barrier, each time you are forced to overcome an obstacle, you grow stronger for the next one. Every challenge will directly contribute to your ability to grow as a problem solver. If you allow yourself to learn from all the obstacles and challenges that are in front of you, your life will be enriched greatly. Just as discomfort is nothing more than an indicator that change is happening, so obstacles are nothing more than an opportunity for growth.

A problem solver's mindset is to look at challenges as ways for them to grow stronger. If they encounter something they can't readily solve, they grow excited at the prospect to learn something new. You can learn so much from these challenges in your life if you start to look at them as good things instead of frustrations. All it takes is a measured, focused decision to adopt a new pattern of thinking, one that looks at challenges as necessary for growth instead of something to avoid.

Step Three: Run Toward Challenges

If you want to learn how to embrace challenges and become like a problem solver, then you must make the conscious effort to seek out challenges and struggles wherever you can. Building your desire to tackle a challenge head on is similar to working out a muscle. Just as you must exercise a muscle many times to make it stronger, so must you focus on seeking out challenge wherever you can in order to build the mindset of someone who is a problem solver.

What are some practical ways that you can learn to embrace challenge? Well the first step is to make the decision that you are going to seek out hardship wherever you can, so that you can build that initial reflex.

Consider the rain for a moment. What is oftentimes our reaction when it begins to rain outside? We become concerned with walking out in it, despite the fact that rain just makes us uncomfortable. Barring any serious safety issues, there's nothing that rain can do to us except make us feel a little bit wet. Someone who's looking to build up their strength and willingness to overcome challenges might see the rain as a chance to engage in a safe, accessible test of will in the face adversity. They will walk through a heavy rainstorm and endure the temporary discomfort of being cold and wet.

We will be listing out a few different ideas for how you can make a daily point of seeking out hardship and challenge in order to grow stronger. But remember, it's as much of a mindset as it is an action. You must cultivate the desire to be willing to engage in difficulty in order to be able to solve the problems better in your life.

Here are some ways that you can seek out adversity in your life:

- Take the stairs instead of the elevator. The further the stairs are, the better!

- Make a point to speak your mind when dealing with other people, don't start unnecessary fights but be willing to disagree with people in a civil manner.

- Take a cold shower every day for a week. In a comfort driven world, this can be an extremely effective way to learn how to push past discomfort.

- Workout in a regular manner in such a way that challenges you each time, forcing you to push past your comfort zone.

- When you have choices to choose between something that's easy and something that's hard, take the hard option.

Adapting the mindset of the problem solver is necessary if you're looking to be able to effectively find solutions to the things in your life that challenge you. It's not enough to simply learn how to solve a single problem, because throughout the rest of your life you're going to encounter difficulty, hardship and struggle. By adapting the mindset of the problem solver you can have an extremely sharp axe that will allow you to cut down any problem in front of you.

Chapter 3: The Discovery Process of Problem Solving

Alright, so we've spent a good amount of time talking about how to approach a problem when you're feeling overwhelmed and we've discussed how to develop the mindset of a problem solver. Let's look at the next section of problem solving: The Discovery Process.

Remember, these steps are to be applied to just about any problem that you encounter. Discovery is the process of sifting through the necessary data to determine what your options are. In other words, it is analyzing what the problem is and taking a look at all of the possible solutions. Critical thinking, objectivity and good judgment are required when it comes to the discovery process. Let's take a look at each component in detail and then look at some practical ways we can learn to use discovery in conjunction with problem solving.

Critical Thinking:

Critical thinking is the ability to gather data and make a decision based purely off of that data. It involves research, study, verification and ultimately application of the data gathered.

In terms of problem solving, critical thinking allows for you to gather information relevant to your problem and interpret the value of it. One example of critical thinking is actually rather automatic. Going back to the example of the flat tire problem: if you had a flat tire your brain would automatically begin to retrieve any relevant data relating to a flat tire. It would begin to interpret experiences and inform you of what you know about the situation.

As discussed before, if you don't have sufficient information on the situation at hand, you won't be able to solve the problem easily. Critical thinking is an extremely important skill to have in the process of problem solving.

So how do we improve our critical thinking ability? Well you can do it by:

- Reflecting more on your day and thinking through the choices you have made. By focusing on becoming more aware of your thought processes, you will be able to make better decisions in the future.

- Be open minded about information. Rather than holding to one viewpoint, it's far better to look at both sides of a discussion and learn how to see the truth. Each time you analyze an argument and objectively look for truth, you are building your ability to sort through information.

- Stop when making a decision and really look at all of the factors involved. Many times we tend to let our automatic decision making processes make the choice for us, so instead of thinking critically we just default to options and decisions that we are used to.

- Learn to question assumptions that are being proposed to you. Especially when you're in the decision making process of solving a problem, assumptions can often be present without being challenged. By learning to look for assumptions and learning to question the validity of them, you will boost your critical thinking skills for certain.

Objectivity:

When we are looking at the discovery process, we must realize that we often take our own biases into the situation. A bias is a prejudice against a person or thing that often comes from either a negative understanding or from a negative experience. Don't discount how powerful biases can be when it comes to problem solving. If you aren't careful, a bias could quickly ruin your goals to have a solution to a problem.

Let's look at an example where bias can come into play when it comes to problem solving. Suppose that someone is trying to solve their financial situations. They are trying to use the discovery process to gather data on possible solutions. In the process of their search they come across a finance book that claims to have the solution to their debt problem. This individual says "Well I know that the Johnson's bought that book and it didn't work for them, so there's no way it'll work for me." This individual allowed their bias to prevent themselves from using a resource which very well could hold the answer to their problems.

    We must be willing to look at all sources of information without letting our biases creep in. We are, of course, to use discernment and caution when it comes to believing these sources of information. But we cannot discount them just because of how we feel about the source material. An argument against the person instead of the information provided is known as an Ad Hominem attack. These are logical fallacies where we disagree with something on the person instead of on the points. Ad Hominem is usually one of the primary types of biases we can experience when we are sifting through new information. Disagreeing with a fact because you don't like the political stance of the person providing the fact is allowing your biases to get the best of you.

We are all biased in some degree. It's natural for us to have the ideas that we agree with and to be suspicious of anyone different from our point of view. But when we make the conscious effort to shelve how we feel and instead focus on what we can learn, we are opening ourselves up to information and data that we wouldn't normally look for. This can give us an advantage when it comes to being able to look at every possible solution in problem solving.

Judgment:

The final element of the discovery is learning how to have good judgment. When you are in the process of sorting through facts, ideas and concepts, it's important to be able to see what is true and tell what is false. In essence, you rely on your ability to judge in just about any situation where you have to decide between more than one outcome.

What are the things that make up good judgment? Let's take a look:

- **Big Picture Thinking**: When you have to make a decision, it is extremely beneficial to consider the long term effects of such a choice. Oftentimes we can get bogged down in the minutia of details and only see the trees instead of the whole forest. Good judgment allows for us to focus on the whole of the problem instead of just one detail.

- **Thinking Realistically**: If something seems too good to be true, it most likely is. A person with good judgment skills often looks for the drawback in a solution, knowing that most everything is some kind of trade off.

- **Gut Decisions**: Sometimes something might feel off. This is our natural sense of intuition. It is our brain's ability to subconsciously put together information and signal to us that something is wrong without us explicitly knowing what is wrong. Sometimes it can be extremely beneficial to trust your gut instinct and remain cautious. You shouldn't make a serious decision just off of a feeling, but you can let those feelings give you some extra level of discernment.

- **Skepticism**: Being overly skeptical isn't good, but having a healthy dose of skepticism in your daily thinking can assist you with making the right choices. Just because someone says something is true doesn't necessarily mean it is true.

- **Look for Proof:** A good judge is someone who looks for proof. If a man claiming that he has a revolutionary system to get out of debt has no proof, is poor himself and those who use his system are also poor, chances are the system doesn't work so great. Trust but verify is a great policy to have in place when it comes to taking in independent information on a potential problem solver.

So with these three elements discussed, it's now time to look at a step-by-step process in which the discovery process is utilized. We will be showing you a series of actions that you can take when you begin to look at how to solve your problem. You must go slowly here, if you're looking for a quick fix to solve your problem, you are still focusing on just learning how to fix a specific problem instead of learning to adapt to a problem solver mindset.

Discovery Process Step One: Get the Facts

Assuming that you've broken down your problem into as many pieces as it can go, it's time for you to work on gathering all of the facts that you have available at your disposal. Write down everything that you know about the situation, don't leave anything out. For example, if one of your major problems is that your dryer isn't working properly and you aren't sure what to do, you would write a list out somewhat like this:

Fact: The Dryer isn't working

Fact: It was just fixed last week

Fact: When I try to run the dryer, it begins making a strange wheezing noise

Fact: The dryer is A Whirlpool Duet

Regardless of what the problem is, if you're looking to overcome it, you must be able to write out all of the facts that are in play. This is going to help you significantly when you begin to gather data, which is the next step.

Discovery Process Step Two: Put Together a List of Sources of Information

Once you know what the problem is, you need to compile a central database of all the possible solutions. You must be able to know where to go for such information. For example, if you were working on fixing the dryer you would have a list of different sources of assistance in learning on solutions.

Source 1: The Internet

Source 2: The mechanic who worked on the dryer last week

Source 3: The whirlpool manual

Source 4: The Whirlpool help hot-line

Source 5: My neighbor who's a mechanic.

By putting together, a comprehensive list of things that may potentially offer solutions, you are then able to effectively go through that list and begin gathering information on how to actually solve your problem. Please note that the discovery process is still just about educating yourself as much as possible, the third phase, the action phase, is where we will actually begin to go about solving the problem. When you choose to build the good habits of getting as educated as possible about each major problem that you face, you will be setting yourself up to live life as a problem solver!

Discovery Process Step Three: Gathering Possible Solutions

The final step in the discovery process is putting together all of the solutions that you have come across and then working on an action plan. It might be tempting to find a solution, then try it and see it if it works one solution at a time, but this can be cumbersome and will slow you down if the first three solutions that you come across don't work.

It is more effective to be able to sit down and gather up all of the solutions that you have found, evaluate each one and then determine the order in which you will work with them. This will allow you to get fully educated on the problem and will allow for your approach to be quick and adaptive. If something doesn't work out, rather than having to go all the way back to step two, you can just go down the list to the next solution that you learned.

Here's what that list might look like if we continue using the dryer example:

Solution 1: Check the door switch to see if it's working properly

Solution 2: Unplug the dryer and test the thermal fuse

Solution 3: Call the repairman and ask for his services

Solution 4: Get a new dryer

Each solution here is ordered in such a way where the easiest solution is proposed first and then each solution after that grows more complex. By using a simple, straightforward approach to gathering information, taking inventory of the solutions and then putting together an action plan, you can learn to solve problems quickly and easily.

But what if the problems are a bit more complicated than just a broken down dryer? Well, that's where the third phase comes into place: the action phase. Let's go ahead and move onto the next chapter where we will take a look at both long-term strategy and plan implementation.

Chapter 4: Taking Action

As mentioned earlier, there are three distinct phases to problem solving. Approach leads us to look at the problem for what it is. It allows us to identify what the problem is and lets us break it down into several smaller problems. Discovery then allows for us to gather information and possible solutions about the problem and put them into a plan of action. The third part, is the action phase and that is where we will actually implement the solutions that we have discovered.

This might come as a surprise, but having the solution to your problem figured out doesn't actually mean that you will solve your problem. In fact, it can be said that there are thousands of obvious solutions to our problems in life, but the biggest problem is that we don't do any of them.

Consider a person who is trying to lose weight. There are, in fact, easily acquirable solutions that are guaranteed to work when it comes to solving this problem. When a person eats less, exercises routinely and makes sure to consume an appropriate amount of protein, fats and carbohydrates to their age and weight level, they will lose weight. Yet, if we look at the dieting industry we can see that there are millions of people who are still struggling with weight loss despite the ease at which getting a meal plan or a workout plan is possible. The problem doesn't lie in education here, rather the problem lies in implementation.

Knowing the right answer doesn't necessarily mean that you will follow all of the steps. So, we're going to spend some time really breaking down how to take a plan and turn it into action.

Implementation Step One: Develop a Strategy

The first step to being able to implement your plan for solving a problem is developing a strategy of how you want to handle it. In general, you don't really need a strategy for short term problems, such as fixing things. But, in long-term problems such as reducing debt, going back to college, getting a job at a new firm or navigating through a divorce, you're going to want to have a strategy.

A strategy is different from a list of solutions. A list of solutions will simply show you where you want to go. A strategy is what tells you how you're going to get there. For example, if you're working to get out of debt, you might have a few solutions such as: get a higher paying job, sell your car and buy a cheaper car, refinance a loan. All of those solutions are useful, but they require more than just one step. When you take your list of solutions and begin to figure out how you are going to implement them, you are developing a strategy.

A strategy speaks in extreme specifics. It has specific goals and objectives. For example, if you're developing a strategy on how to get out of debt, you'd take each solution and begin to outline just exactly how and when you're going to achieve such a plan. Let's look at the example below:

Solution 1: Get a higher paying Job

- Apply for a job at Jones Law Firm by Friday
- Ask for a raise on Monday
- Call contact at old job

By placing some tangibles in your strategy, you are able to move toward a specific goal as opposed to having some vague idea of what it looks like to handle the problem. The more complex your problems are, the more of a defined strategy you'll need to have in order to tackle them. Don't be discouraged by the idea that in order to have a good implementation you need to work on a good strategy. Rather you should embrace the idea fully and work to put together strategies that will aid you in solving your problems.

What are some ways to build a good strategy? Well, let's look at a few basic strategy building tips.

Strategy Tip One: Be Specific

When developing a strategy, it is extremely important to be specific with each step. Your discovery phase has already provided you with solutions necessary to get to work, all you need to do is focus on getting the specifics down. The more focused you are and the more detail oriented your strategy is, the more you will get done.

Strategy Tip Two: Have Milestones

A milestone is a kind of sub-goal that keeps track of your overall progress. When you set up a milestone you are creating a tangible goal to reach. Essentially something that you can move towards as you work to solve your problems. The number of milestones needed to complete a project are basically up to you. Keep in mind that milestones shouldn't be too big and there shouldn't be too much time in between completing them.

Strategy Tip Three: Have Due Dates

A due date on each milestone will help you in your quest to work toward the completion of your goals. The pressure that a deadline provides will push you forward in your desire to take action in solving your problems. A vague idea of "someday I'll pay down my debt" can be defeated quite easily. The human brain does not work well with abstract ideas. The concept of "someday" just isn't real enough for it to feel motivated by. When you think in terms of "By next month I will have paid off my first credit bill," the concept becomes more concrete and more attainable. This in turn leads you to having a better chance of taking action.

Strategy Tip Four: Write it Down!

A good strategy isn't just something that you should have in your head. It is very difficult to keep track of all the plans, ideas and milestones that you will have for your strategy. So by making a point to write it down, you are setting yourself up for success. Write everything down, put a due date next to it and then get to work! Let's move onto the next implementation tip.

Implementation Step Two: Consistency is Key

If you're going to be a problem solver, then you're going to need to have a mindset of being consistent in working toward your goal of solving your problems. Consistency is key when it comes to getting the work required to solve the problem done. If you aren't consistent then any solution or plan that you have won't be accomplished because you aren't spending the time necessary to get the work done.

Consider if you are trying to solve a debt problem. The only way to solve a debt problem is to consistently earn money and pay off the debt. If you pay a little bit here and there, you won't ever be able to eliminate that problem.

Some tasks, especially the shorter ones, don't really need consistency, but when it comes to solving long term problems, if you aren't dedicated then you might be in serious trouble!

So what are some ways that you can be consistent? Let's take a look:

Consistency Tip 1: Work Every Day

Even if it's just reviewing the strategy or looking for more solutions, if you choose to work every day toward solving your problem it will get done much quicker than if you give it only a few hours every other week or so. Make a point to spend some time. The bigger the problem is, the more time you are going to want to give it, but make a point to spend time on it every single day.

Consistency Tip 2: Make a Schedule

If you have a busy life and there are so many things that threaten your time, having a set schedule for time to work on your problem can be extremely effective in giving you the necessary space to write your strategy. By keeping a set time that you work on your project each day or each week, you will grow more consistent in being able to actually work on your problems.

Consistency Tip 3: Enlist Assistance

As discussed before, there can be enormous benefit to having help from others when it comes to getting a problem solved. If you're someone who struggles to be consistent with working on your problem, whatever it may be, then perhaps you would do better if you found someone who would be willing to help you work on it. Look for an accountability partner who can check in on your status and hold you to your deadlines. You may also find someone who will be willing to help you solve the problem.

It never hurts to pull someone else in when working to overcome a problem. When you make the choice to bring in additional help, you are essentially doubling your capacity to work. One person can only do one thing at a time, so when you bring in a second person, you are essentially increasing your efficiency by 100%.

Implementation Step Three: Learn the Practice of Kaizen

If you want to learn to take action, but struggle when you see the monumental tasks required to overcome your problems, you might want to consider learning how to implement the practice of Kaizen.

What is Kaizen? It's Japanese for change for the better. It is a philosophy based around the idea of continuous, small improvements in life that over time lead to major changes. The concept of Kaizen began after World War II, when Japanese businessmen were confronted with the reality that they had to rebuild a war-torn country that had suffered from extensive damage. Rather than look at the entirety of a destroyed factory and try to tackle everything at once, they instead began to develop the philosophy of trying to fix what they could one day a time.

Kaizen is a problem solver's mindset; it is not a simple solution to a problem but it is an approach that will allow for you to continuously change as you begin to work towards fixing your goal.

Let's take a look at a series of principles that make up the philosophy of Kaizen:

Kaizen Philosophy Component 1: A Little Bit Every Day

The philosophy of Kaizen can best be summed up as 1% change every day. The idea is that by making a small series of changes over time, you will eventually grow better and better with each passing day. So suppose that you had to pay off a major debt. The principle of Kaizen would say that it would be better to pay 1% off of that debt every single day, or at least pay whatever can be paid each day until eventually over time the entire debt is paid off.

Small improvements eventually end up leading to significant changes over time. When you adopt the mindset of looking for how you can improve your predicament or solve your problem each day by just a little, you will eventually find that the problem has been reduced to a very manageable size. Instead of allowing your workload or the size of the problem to overwhelm you, Kaizen allows for you to turn your workload into manageable bite sized pieces.

Kaizen Philosophy Component 2: Look for the Things You Can Do

In problem solving there is often the temptation to look at the things that we are not able to do. We become fixated on the big problem. When we see that our house needs to be repaired due to damage from a storm, we look at all the things that require serious machinery, heavy lifting or construction teams. When we face a major obstacle like improving our education we see the cost of tuition loom over us, convincing us we'll never get to where we want to go.

The Kaizen philosophy is one where we choose to focus on the small things that we can do each day rather than focus on the whole problem at once. If you're trying to put money away for school, chances are you can't just earn the $40,000 in a single day. But, you can make a point to apply for a scholarship every day or work on a freelance job that will provide you with money.

The Kaizen strategy depends upon the recognition that gradual, steady change will greatly improve your situation. By focusing on what you can do each day and dedicating yourself to working on that, you will eventually fix your problems without much of a major expenditure of energy. This works great especially if you're someone who might be prone to fatigue or exhaustion when working to achieve your goals.

Kaizen Philosophy Component 3: Patience

One of the biggest things that can disrupt any long term plan or strategy to deal with a problem is the lack of patience. After committing to a strategy, the monotony of sticking to the same plan or the feeling that it is going too slow might end up causing us to abandon the plan prematurely. Once this plan is abandoned, we are slowed down significantly as we are then forced to come up with a new plan. Sometimes we might just abandon the strategy without developing a new strategy.

Kaizen is an approach to the long haul of problem solving. Likewise, it requires the utmost patience to be able to work toward solutions with a slow, measured approach. Patience is a virtue however, as no major plan is ever finished quickly. Choosing to adopt a mindset of patience will allow for you to work at a sustainable pace in solving your problems. The keyword is sustainable. There are many strategies that can be developed that push you too hard. Sometimes these extremely aggressive strategies can help you get things done quickly and effectively, but they often take a great deal of focus, concentration and energy. Eventually your energy or interest level will decrease due to the intensity of the program and there will be a loss of efficiency along the way. It's far better to take it slow and steady than to burn out at the beginning of the project.

Kaizen Philosophy Component 4: The Tide Washes Over Mistakes

Suppose that if you're working to solve your problems you make a few mistakes. Maybe you missed a day in your diet, perhaps you lost the funding that you needed to refinance your credit or maybe you just simply didn't work to solve your problem. What is the typical reaction to when we make mistakes? We often feel as if we blew it and we can't come back from it. Sometimes we grow despondent or frustrated to the point where we might even give up.

With Kaizen, keeping the mindset of progressive, slow changes will naturally offset your own mistakes with each passing day. The tide will essentially wash over your mistakes. This means that the amount of progress that you do over the course of a year will easily erase a single day's worth of failings. If you can't stick to your diet plan one day out of seven, you still have six days of success. Kaizen is meant to allow for you to progressively grow each day rather than focus on big gains at a time. If you are working to fix your house and you end up doing a little bit of damage or break something of value, you can always keep focusing on the thing that needs repairs, keeping with the Kaizen philosophy. Rather than allow for your mistakes to hold you hostage, you can instead focus on continuing forward, improving each day just by a little bit. Eventually you will find that those mistakes won't compare to the sheer amount accomplished by a progressive, daily increase.

Kaizen isn't based on immediacy, which means that even once you reach your goals if you continue to practice the goal of adding small improvements each day, you will go above and beyond what you were setting out to do.

Don't let mistakes slow you down as you work to progressively improve yourself and work through your problems. Keep to it and each day that you succeed you will find that you are closer and closer to your goals. This philosophy is meant for those who want to develop more than just a simple system for problem solving. This philosophy is for those who want to live a life as a problem solver.

Kaizen is certainly one of the most effective techniques you can learn when it comes to problem solving because when you learn it, you can live it out for the rest of your life. Taking all aspects of improvement, whether it's solving a money problem, working on a health issue or focusing on improving your relationships, the slow 1% increase approach will greatly lead to change and prosperity in your life. Let's move onto the final step when it comes to implementation.

Implementation Step Four: Action

The final and most important step in learning how to implement your strategies, plans and ideas is quite simply just to take action. At the end of the day, no amount of planning, strategizing or daydreaming will actually get your work done. Once you have figured out the solutions to your problems, you must put your plans into place and get to work. There is nothing that replaces a spirit of action. Taking action is more than just doing something, it's also a mindset that is necessary to develop. When you plan to do something, don't just put if off until tomorrow, if possible take care of it today. Make a point of going through your whole to-do list every morning or evening and see what you can get done right then and there. Don't give into the temptation to rest when it's not time to rest and certainly don't think that you can do it tomorrow.

Procrastination is the enemy of action and it will do whatever it can to convince you to wait until tomorrow, or next week. The fact is, when it comes to taking action, tomorrow never really comes. There will always be an excuse to wait until tomorrow. Don't give in to the pressure to wait. There is only the present when it comes to being a problem solver.

All of the things that we have talked about are tools to help you reach a point where you can solve problems steadily and quickly. If you find that you have read the book, memorized the processes and tried to adapt the mindset of a problem solver, but still aren't taking action then it will all have been for nothing. In the end, even a bad plan will accomplish more when put into action as opposed to a plan that is perfect but is never implemented. You have what it takes to get it done, all you really need to do is commit to getting it done!

Conclusion:

At the end of the day, we must embrace the fact that our problems will never truly cease to plague us. When one problem ends, another will often show up. The goal isn't to live a life free of problems, rather the goal is to learn how to overcome these challenges. No matter what, our lives will be filled with conflict, challenges and obstacles that must be overcome. In order to overcome these obstacles, we must develop a new mindset. One that is welcoming of struggle and is comfortable when looking at serious problems. We must make a point to develop the mindset of a problem solver.

It's not easy changing our thinking either. The process of changing our minds from accepting comfort and rejecting discomfort can be hard but in the end it's extremely worth it. A problem solver doesn't look to keep themselves safe, rather they seek to push themselves towards reaching their goals.

A problem solver learns to use a system of approach, discovery and action in order to break through any problem. They are patient and focused, knowing that it takes a lot of work to get through the problem at hand. They don't look for ways to solve a single problem, rather a problem solver develops a system that will allow them to approach any problem and solve it easily.

As you begin your journey to make the transformation into becoming a problem solver, keep in mind that this is a process that is meant to take time. Be patient with yourself and focus on learning how to adapt to anything in your way. Remember, don't just solve a single problem, change your mind and adapt to become a problem solver!

Other books available by Michael Sloan on Kindle, paperback and audio:

The Art of Thinking Big: How to Establish and Reach Your Goals, Be Successful and Achieve Anything You Want In Life

The Art of Public Speaking: How to Speak In Front of an Audience without Fear

Positive Thinking with Action: How to Fight Back Against Negative Thought Patterns and Win at Life

Made in the USA
Lexington, KY
26 August 2019